REALTOR RESCUE

How to be a Realtor and Still Have a Life

Praise For This Book

"One of our most experienced brokers has created a guide for staying happy in our challenging industry.... Brava!"

Candace Adams, President & CEO, Berkshire Hathaway Home Services New England

"With 38 successful years in real estate, Sandi Klein has written a unique, must-read book. She illustrates how to maximize pleasure and avoid the pitfalls of working in a demanding profession. Her refreshing style makes this fun."

Fran Koenig, President, Fran Koenig Associates

"This easy read offers personal stories and tips to address the independent contractor's quest for work-life balance."

Dipti Joshi, MD, MBA, CPT

Realtor Rescue

First published in 2014 by
Panoma Press

48 St Vincent Drive, St Albans, Herts, AL1 5SJ, UK

info@panomapress.com
www.panomapress.com

Book layout by Charlotte Mouncey
Printed on acid-free paper from managed forests.

ISBN 978-1-909623-61-3

REALTOR RESCUE

How to be a Realtor and Still Have a Life

Sandi Klein

I dedicate this book to the memory of Manny Klein, accomplished writer, playwright, and inspiration.

Acknowledgements

Thank you to the following people who were instrumental in my creation and execution of this work. Their help has made this an enjoyable and productive venture for me, and has enriched the content and style of the book.

Michele Sacco, Simona Barcelo Casarini, Sandy Soule, Myron Kerstetter, Mindy Gibbins-Klein, Francine Koenig, Candace Adams, Eric Bjork, Phil Lohmeyer, Dipti Joshi, Harvey Thomas, Marilyn Harris, Brian Buffini, Liz Fox, and Michele Johnson.

Illustrations by Phil Lohmeyer

Contents

Acknowledgements   9

Why Realtor Rescue?   13

Chapter 1: Name Your Poison   21

Chapter 2: You Are The Brand Name   31

Chapter 3: For Sellers - My Home Is My Castle   39

Chapter 4: Be The Captain Of Your Ship   51

Chapter 5: There Are Positive Negatives   61

Chapter 6: Make It The Time Of Your Life   75

Chapter 7: The Family Is All In   87

Chapter 8: Forget Me Not   99

Chapter 9: Avoid The April Showers   109

Chapter 10: Ready, Set, Goal   117

Chapter 11: Play Nicely   125

Afterword: What's Next?   131

About the Author   133

Why Realtor Rescue?

How long has it been since you were able to relax in your success and just daydream? How long since you've had a really long soak in the bathtub and just lazed in the tub for so long that you had to add more hot water because you were in there for almost an hour? Have you been able to cuddle up with your spouse or significant other and allow phone calls and emails to go unanswered because you turned the volume off and are just reveling in the warmth and love of your closeness?

By this time in your reading, you are probably wondering what planet I live on that could ask these questions, knowing that the answers are going to be "never", "seldom", or "maybe once in a while". How sad, but true, that most of us in the real estate profession have lost that innocent, sky-high sense of joy and the ability to capture the spirit of our old life – before kids, before responsibilities, before CLIENTS! I have been there, lived it, suffered for years with it, and said so many times, "When do I get time for ME?"

For a bit of background information on my life, I have been a Realtor in Greenwich, Connecticut for 38 years. I came to this profession after 11 years of teaching English in high schools in New York. I married young, right after my first year of teaching. We had our first child in that year of marriage, and I returned to teaching a year after that. Our second child was born 2 ½ years after the first one, and I had to continue in graduate school one night a week to get the required Masters degree for high school teaching certification. I guess you could say that my life was "frontloaded", like a stock purchase. Luckily, I was very young and very healthy, and I had a wonderfully cooperative husband who was also a teacher, so we could share the child rearing after a long day of teaching.

As much as I had some help from him and from a baby sitter, I frequently felt that I was in perpetual motion, like a hamster on a wheel in a cage. It was like "Stop the world; I want to get off!" So, I do know the feeling of constantly being at the mercy of others, and never getting time to do the things I used to love doing. How could I take a long walk? How could I watch TV? I had quizzes and papers to grade, lessons to plan, books to re-read in preparation for my five teaching classes a day. Then my own children were getting farther along in school and I had to be sure they were doing their homework, taking baths, eating properly, and enjoying their lives and activities. A typical day's activities would start with greeting the baby sitter early in the morning, driving to work as a teacher, spending seven hours at work, going food shopping for the family, getting school supplies for the kids, possibly getting clothing for them, keeping doctor appointments for them, driving them to piano or dance lessons, religious school carpools, and keeping play dates for them.

Whew!! It was pretty intense in those days. I did all that for 11 years, and then I entered the real estate profession. (Oh, did I mention that I also had to study for the real estate exam and take 30 hours of coursework in Real Estate Principles and Practices, all while finishing my last year of teaching that June?)

Do you get the idea that I know what you're going through, that I've "been there and done that"?

So why have I chosen to write this book *now*? I guess I look around me and see so many of my colleagues harried, nervous, fragmented, getting no relief, and worried about not knowing when their next sale will come. This is even harder than being a teacher because, at least in that job, you knew what you would earn each month.

More worrisome, I also see co-workers losing faith in themselves, and starting to think that this profession is not what they thought it would be. Even if the money is not that important, the sense of self -fulfillment is. I see people who never smile unless someone has just told a joke. There's never a smile on their faces just walking into the office. Instead, a frazzled, self-absorbed misery emanates from many of my fellow Realtors, not just sometimes, but usually. I have actually had people ask me why I'm always whistling, always seeming happy. Well, I have my reasons for that, and I have some remedies for the hang-dog looks on some of my beleaguered associates' faces.

And that brings me to the motivation for writing this book and calling it *Realtor Rescue*. You see, I truly believe that I can help to rescue anyone in the real estate business who has become disillusioned and dissatisfied, successful yet harried, with no life. If you see yourself in the following pages, that is the first step. If you can take some of the well-intentioned advice from "one of your own" who has "been there and done that", then read on.

I didn't mention this before, but I owned a successful "boutique" real estate office in Greenwich for 14 years before selling it to a large "chain". Even by doing that sale of the company, I was starting to shed some of the stress in my life that comes with having to be responsible for between 15 and 24 agents at any one time. That responsibility and the constant overseeing of the staff and the agents made for a very stressful life. Throw in the litigiousness of the real estate environment with the threat of whimsical lawsuits, and you can see that the fun factor was ebbing every day that I was in that ownership position. When we sold to the large multi-office chain we simply had to become agents again, and the burden was lessened a little bit each day. Now I could get back into just listing and selling homes for my clients, and begin to enjoy the things that had attracted me to the business in the first place.

I am rooting for you! I want to see more smiles, fewer headaches and other stress-induced ailments, and

I want to see more fulfilling personal relationships around me.

Enjoy, and, if you see yourself here in these pages, I've succeeded in my goals.

Now.... are you ready to accomplish some of your goals (even if you don't yet know what those goals are)?

Name Your Poison

CHAPTER ONE

Chapter 1: Name Your Poison

A common complaint that I've heard almost every Realtor say at one point or another is, "This client is driving me crazy!" This sentiment can surface after one meeting with the client or, also, after months, or even years, of working with this client. I had many of my own agents come to me in tears, and reveal that they are *at their wit's end* and they've been working with the client so hard for over 8 months! My advice was invariably to stop working with that party right now!

Often the agent would say, "But I've been working with them day and night for over 8 months! I've done everything for them!" My response was always, "Do you want to spend another 8 months in the same way?" Then the agent would look puzzled and say, "I don't have to call them back? I don't have to keep working with them?' I would counsel them to drop the client, and say, "There is someone really nice, right around the corner, who needs you, and you have spent all of your time and energy on this toxic client and you have nothing left to give this new, deserving client, because all of your strength, spirit, and enthusiasm has been used up in this futile relationship."

What kind of toxicity do these difficult clients exhibit?

First, let's talk about the prospective buyers....

One agent I know had "buyers" who greeted her at every meeting with a list of 20 homes found on Zillow, Trulia, Realtor.com, the New York Times, and the local newspaper and insisted on seeing them all. This person needed to be "in charge", and refused to whittle down the list. The agent served as a taxi driver, ferrying the couple to every home the client had on the list. Time and energy were wasted every visit, resulting in the agent starting to feel that she wasn't very effective. (Hint: your enthusiasm and optimistic attitude are mandatory for having a long life in this business, and any client who makes you feel bad about yourself should be dropped as soon as possible.) Instead of taking the lead from the agent and letting her map out the showing schedule, this buyer was demanding to see everything advertised everywhere.

I had an equally demeaning experience with a client from another country who was in a very high price range. This was a woman whose family owned a chain of department stores on the scale of Macy's. She was used to many servants, and, I guess, she was going to include me in that list. I was being honored at an annual luncheon given at holiday time by my firm. I told the client that I could see her any other time, but she insisted that we go during the time of this special event. I obliged and left the luncheon, changing out of my dress shoes and into snow boots to take her to the property she wanted to see. This, by the way, was the same client who had kept me waiting on former visits for at least 30 minutes each time, and that day was no exception. Needless to say, she did not buy the property, went back to her country half way across the world, and never bought a home in the U.S. This wasn't all bad; at least it taught me that when I have an important occasion to participate in, I do not cancel it or leave it before the main event takes place. If it was important enough for me to schedule in the first place, it's important enough for me not to cancel.

Because of mandated buyer brokerage in the state where I work, it is illegal to show any home listed by another firm without having a Buyer Representation form signed by the prospective buyer. What do you do if the buyer refuses to sign this form? Your first question has to be, "Why is that?" If he says, "I don't sign anything at a first meeting," that's fair enough, but you don't want to risk your license by showing homes illegally, and you don't want to be restricted to showing only those homes listed by your own company, do you?

A solution I have found is to say lightly, "Today it's like we are on a first date. I will therefore list the homes we are seeing today, and you can sign the form that says for these homes only, I represent you as your Buyer Broker. If we get along and want to go out again, we are going to 'go steady', and you can sign a blanket agreement that I will represent you for all the homes you see in our town." It may take a little time to list all of the homes you are showing on that first visit, but at least you are protected and are working legally.

(If they refuse to sign even the representation for the specific homes you are seeing on that first meeting, it would be wise to not even let them get into your car!)

Another way toxic clients can erode your confidence and belief in yourself is when they always call at any hour, or demand to see homes on very short notice. Clients can have an inspired idea once in a while, but when this becomes their M.O., this doesn't bode well for you, the agent.

The twin sister of this behavior is the one where the prospective buyer habitually sets up appointments to see you, and then breaks them. How important or skilled can you feel if a person doesn't think enough of you to consider your time to be important? Again, anyone can have an emergency wreak havoc with his scheduled appointment but, when it becomes a regular occurrence, you need to re-evaluate this agent-client relationship.

The overly informed client knows every home on the market, and gives you a "pop quiz" at every meeting. You may have skillfully honed a long list of possibilities so that your showing schedule will have some pattern and purpose, but he or she comes in with 6 more homes that they just got off the internet and they insist on seeing them right now. WHAT TO DO? If this becomes a frequent event, you will eventually be beaten into the ground and begin to doubt your knowledge, skills, and expertise – a formula for failure. You need to establish the showing schedule *before you meet*, and keep some order in the visit. *You* are the expert, and *you* are in charge; *they* are being helped to define and refine their goals, and you are there to help them find a home they love.

If a client makes you feel compelled to anticipate their next challenge, you will start to feel inadequate. They shoot questions at you in rapid fire, and it appears that *they* want to be the smart ones in this experience. They don't even listen to the answers you manage to give, as they are onto the next volley.

If you are nodding your head right now as you are reading this, and recognizing some of your experiences with would-be buyers, it's time to remedy this upside-down relationship. You *do* have a choice, you know. You *can* choose your clients. Doesn't it make sense for the long run to create a client base of people who respect you and look to you for advice and information?

If you think that buyers are the only ones who can become toxic, think again.

Some sellers have their bad habits as well, and it is up to *you* to represent them or not in the sale or rental of their home.

The seller who makes you doubt whether you're strong enough and knowledgeable enough is discourteous and boorish. This is the owner who will not price his home fairly to begin with, who refuses to lower the price as the house lingers on the market, who keeps asking for more and bigger ads, and questions you constantly about the lack of hits from the internet. This is the same seller who sets very restricted showing hours with very complicated and elaborate instructions to follow when at the house.

I think you get the idea now of what it does to your enthusiasm, energy, and ego if you allow toxic clients to remain in charge of your real estate life. This can be and should be a wonderful career if you can really understand what it means to be an independent contractor. If you were a teacher, as I once was, you did not have the choice of whom to teach and what schedule to follow daily. As a teacher, you are an employee; you have to do what you are told to do. If you worked in retail, could you refuse to sell to customers who were rude to you? If you were an employee anywhere, would you be able to pick and choose whom to work with?

The client relationship needs to be personal yet professional for both parties. You may be able to "train" certain clients to play by professional rules and thereby establish a mutually respectful and effective relationship.

Now, just think of the freedom you have in being able to work with people YOU choose to work with. You can be as happy and feel as rewarded as I do in this profession if you could just learn to take care of YOURSELF so that you can take care of those deserving clients out there who need you.

CHAPTER TWO

Chapter 2: You Are The Brand Name

How do you think people identify you in the real estate business? Do they first think *ABC Realty* or *123 Homes*? Do they think *The Firm on XYZ Street* or *The firm with the Cute TV Ad* or *The Firm with the Red and Purple Logo*"?

I'm willing to bet that the clients you have, or wish to have, choose to work with *you,* regardless of where you hang your license. This is not to say that if you are working in a company that cannot supply your clients with the marketing benefits they need or support their buying experience, they will seek you out. What I mean is that *you* are the reason they continue to want your services or, conversely, the reason they leave you for another agent. What can you do to make yourself their expert in this real estate experience, and have them remember you *by name*, and refer their friends and family members to you *by name*?

Your company is your "tent"; you are the independent contractor in that accommodating tent. What does that really mean? How is it different from being an employee at a firm? It's just like having people visit you at your home; they are not coming to see the house or the furnishings but, rather, coming to see *you* and to spend time with *you*. When you fully engage with your clients, they will come back to see *you* and seek your advice and guidance. It is for this reason that I offer some tips on how to make the term "clients for life" not just a slogan but, instead, a reality.

The first reason for understanding this concept is that, in this fluid economy, you might change firms several times over the lifetime of your career, and you want your clientele to follow you. I have been in five companies throughout my years in this business in the same town. I started in a very small agency and learned a great deal from my first broker. After about one year, I moved to a larger firm with more agents and the opportunity to learn from and interact with many of them. About eight years later, I opened my own firm with three other women. My clients knew where to find me, and sought me out, no matter where I was located. I had kept in touch and always featured my name prominently in any correspondence with them.

As things changed in the real estate environment in my town through the years, my remaining business partner and I (the other two partners had left the firm within the first three years) decided to sell our *boutique* firm to a large *chain*. The responsibility of owning a firm in this new challenging and litigious climate was not appealing to us anymore. So, once again, the name of my company changed, but my clients knew where to find *me* at all times. Then, after the obligatory two-year non-compete term, I decided to leave the chain I had sold to and move to another large and successful company in town. Did my longtime clients and friends have any trouble following me or referring business to me? They did not, since the reason they had worked with me was because they related to *me*, not to the place where I hung my license.

In still another potential challenge, the company I had grown to love was sold to another firm after my tenure of about twelve years. I now had to change logos, email signatures, company forms, business cards, and all of the former company-based information. Have I lost my clients over this? Of course not, since I have consistently maintained my own identity throughout my thirty+ years in the business and have maintained contact with my key former clients.

One of the best things about being a real estate agent is that you do have the status of independent contractor. Not only is it an advantage for tax purposes, but it frees you to craft a life that suits you, enriches you, and allows you to be the special human being that you are. You can schedule your own hours and are not mandated to put in any set number of hours or abide by any schedule set by anyone but *you*.

This flexibility allows you to enjoy your life by engaging in activities you love and fulfilling any other responsibilities you may have. For instance, many agents go to yoga or exercise classes. Others enjoy crafts, book groups, and bridge. Many join PTA groups in their children's schools, or join a sports activity or a church or synagogue committee.

Have you ever thought about how lucky you are to be able to indulge yourself in these inspiring ventures and not have to keep "regular hours"? Of course, an ancillary result of being active outside of the office is that the people you meet at these activities, and work with, get to know *you*. They get to see the "human" side of you. They come to trust you. They may get to be your clients or refer their family and friends to you. They have seen you as a real person, not just a suit at a desk.

Are you taking advantage of this privilege? Are you counting your blessings every day that you have this freedom to create a life for yourself, along with your business responsibilities?

One thing that will help you love your life in the real estate profession is to recognize what you *don't* like to do, or what drags you down when you have to do it? For instance, not everyone is a born writer. If I'm advising you to stay in touch with your clients, but you hate to write, what do you do? How about having to write ad copy or brochure copy for your listings? Do you hate making charts or Excel sheets, or amassing data to keep your clients informed? The answer is so simple:

Hire someone to do this for you. It can be a bartering or a paid task, but, at the very least, it frees *you* from having to do it! As a good example, I love to write, and have used my talent in the field to write copy for print ads and brochures for listing agents in my firm. I get paid a set amount and fill each request, and the agent is relieved of a piece of their business that he doesn't have to agonize over. He has the time and energy to spend on the things that lift his spirit and make him more productive, instead of sapping him each time he has to do something he is so uneasy about. Can you envision yourself becoming unburdened by finding someone to do the parts of your job that you don't like to do or don't have the talent for?

All of this is part of structuring your life in this profession so that you love your work, and you love your clients. I talked about the "toxic" clients in the last chapter. Now it is time to *brand* yourself, and help your potential clients and longtime clients see you as the well rounded, upbeat person you want to be.

You are the star! There is no other individual who is exactly like you, and you do not have to fit into a company mold. Enjoy your freedom to soar, to style your life in your unique way, and to attract people to you because of your joy.

For Sellers:

My Home Is My Castle

CHAPTER THREE

Chapter 3: For Sellers - My Home Is My Castle

One of the most personal things clients may have to deal with is parting with their home. Choice of a title for this chapter is no mistake, and not to be taken lightly. I have dealt with many hundreds of sellers in my long career, and I can tell you that, with the exception of investors, most clients really deal with separation issues when they decide (or are forced) to sell their home. They dwell on nostalgic factors like all of their children who were born in this house, family dinners around the dining room table, how they worked for months to choose just the right carpeting for the stairs, or the color of the custom paint they had specially mixed for the living room. All of these memories conspire to give them pause about selling their "castle".

When they have fully exhausted all of the emotional reasons for loving their home, they go to the next series of items which may become haggling points in setting the price for their home. They'll enumerate the many improvements they've made and how much each one had cost them. The fact that they've enjoyed the benefits of all of these improvements through the years does not resonate with them. Every cornice and piece of molding must be itemized in their minds and assigned a price tag to raise the price they want to ask for their house.

It is very important for you, as their Realtor, to understand how difficult it is for sellers to be objective about the sale of their precious home. In order to begin the process, you must ask them very specific questions. The answers to these questions will help them (and you) to focus on what this sale means to them, and how easy or difficult handling this project will be for you.

First, ask them WHY they bought this home. Their answer will give you some selling points for marketing if you are hired to be their agent. Next, ask them WHY they are considering putting their home on the market. From the content and phrasing of their answer you will gain insight into how serious they are, and how motivated they are. Many times the answer to this question is "If I can get a good price, I may sell." This will definitely set you up for a rough time, as the owner cannot dictate the price; the market must do that for them. (More about that later)

"WHAT is your timetable?" is an important question, and you will invariably hear, "I'm not in any hurry. If it sells quickly, fine. If not, I'll try again next year." How easy is your job going to be if they can't even envision a practical schedule for themselves, and they don't mind if their home "lingers on the vine" while the market excitement over it withers?

"WHERE are you planning to go?" is a question whose answer is important for you (and for them) to know. If they have a specific goal, such as wanting to retire to Florida or they want to move closer to their out-of-state children, they will focus on that and you can help them do that throughout the time that the house is on the market. This helps them focus on the goal ahead of them, instead of dwelling on their past experiences in their beloved home. Other clients may say that they don't need all the rooms in this house and they've seen a great condo downtown, which will require less maintenance and is less expensive. Still others may have the opposite goal: that of needing more space and hoping to move into a new development in a nearby town with larger homes, which will accommodate their growing family.

Can you see why asking the right questions and listening carefully to the answers will help you to evaluate the urgency level and motivation of your seller clients in getting their home sold?

Now that you think you have a good idea of the background information, how can you direct your sellers and help to influence their behavior before and during the tenure of your listing.

First, and most important, is the pricing of the home. You will be asked (hopefully not told) what is the correct price for this house. Many times, if you are tempted to "buy" the listing, you will give the owner a flatteringly high price, which will influence them to choose you as their Realtor. Warning: Do this at your own peril! Are you ready to "live" with this listing for months, if not years? Will your reputation suffer from inflated priced homes, which languish on the market? How about the time that this will take from your other clients, and from your *other* life outside of real estate? You need to explain to the seller that pricing a home close to the expected selling price will get them a faster sale, and maybe even a final settlement *above* the asking price. If the asking price is wrong, and it is not adjusted regularly, the house will usually sell lower after having been on the market a long time. (Length of time on the market, in itself, is often the reason that a house sells at a lower figure.)

Now that you have tackled the pricing issue, it's sometimes necessary to have the "staging conversation". What does this mean, and how do you do it? It is imperative that you tread very gently through this dialog with your seller, so as not to insult him by criticizing his "castle". The first subject to cover is "Will you be willing to hire a professional stager to really make your home stand out?" You should come to this meeting with photographic examples of "before and after" staging projects. Any good stager should be able to share these photos with you. Staging will usually cost some money up front, but can net the seller a bigger profit in the end, and use up less market time.

Even if they say they don't want to hire a stager, you need to feel able to ask the question "Can you bear to de-clutter and put some of your things in storage or give them to charity?" Again, be gentle; these are the personal belongings of your client, amassed, perhaps, over years, and containing memories. Sometimes, if a home has too little furniture and lacks "oomph", you need to ask if the seller is willing to bring in a few things to "warm up" and "color" the place a bit. This whole topic is fraught with minefields, but it is necessary to have this talk. Do you want to have to market a home that is cluttered, unkempt, or mismatched, and will appeal to no one and will be a nightmare to sell? Wouldn't it be better to use your expertise to make the home more attractive and have it sell well?

If you do decide to take the listing after having the talk about motivation, pricing, and staging (yes, you *do* get to decide whether you want the listing or not!), there are still other issues that could sabotage your marketing.

An agent I know was asked by the three heirs of their parents' estate property to list the home. She was told that two of the heirs lived far away, and the one son who lived nearby would be the one to take care of the details about presentation, showings, and all other things that might come up. She repeatedly asked them to clean up and clear out the house for a more advantageous presentation. They would not agree to have a professional company do this work, and the son who lived nearby could not seem to get the time or energy to do it either. When an offer did come in, the three siblings could not unite on the price or on making a counter offer, often arguing and procrastinating, and eventually refusing to accept the offer.

This listing lasted for about 9 months on the market, with no other serious offers and no more improvements made to the home. After that listing expired, they listed with another agent, at the same price, and finally sold for the price that they had rejected during the first agent's listing. Needless to say, she was disappointed and felt "used", as she was the one who had made some trips to the town recycling area and was also the one who had tried to tidy up and help clean up the house with the heir who lived nearby during her tenure as the listing agent. This is one of the situations common in inherited properties where multiple owners can't seem to agree on anything. The next time you are faced with this type of ownership of a home, be forewarned that it can get pretty messy (pun intended!).

Your seller may want to restrict showing times because he would prefer not to be disturbed too often or at certain times. This seller mandates no late afternoons, no early mornings, and only specific times on weekends. Where is the motivation level of this client? How many more months will it take to sell this home that is rarely available to show? Are they allowing the use of the popular electronic key box for their showing convenience, or do they insist that you, as their listing agent, accompany all buyer agents and their clients? Coordinating time schedules is sometimes tricky, and you may miss many showings because of it. Of course, in cases of luxury homes with intricate security systems and electric gates, this is usually done with the listing agent accompanying.

The foreclosed properties that are listed by the banks that now own them have other conditions that differ from those in "normal" homes. The banks usually sell the homes in "as is" condition, and will not do repairs of any type. One agent in my town told me of a foreclosed listing on which he had an accepted offer and for which the buyers had the building inspection done. Unfortunately, the water and heat had been turned off for the winter, so the buyers could not test them at that time. About a week before the closing, the buyers went in to check the systems that could not be seen during the prior inspection. The plumber who had turned off the heat and water came in to turn them on and, to everyone's surprise and dismay, water started leaking all over the house. The bank refused to pay for this, as they felt that the buyers were getting a very good deal on a house that had sold several years before at 30% higher. The buyers, who were really motivated, and believed they were getting a bargain in the marketplace, agreed to proceed with the purchase. I mention this story as a cautionary tale for agents who list or show foreclosed bank-owned properties. If you have some idea of how this type of sale differs from the usual seller-owned property sale, you may prepare yourself to have a somewhat different experience from what you are used to. They say, "Forewarned is forearmed" because it is true.

Another thing that a listing agent must do is to keep in constant touch with sellers.

Maintaining the data for a listing is something you need to do on a regular basis. Your seller must be apprised of competing new listings in their price range.

Sales of homes in the physical area of the listing, and those in similar price ranges should be reported to the seller immediately for comparison to their offering. The seller needs to be kept abreast at least once a week of how his home fits into the marketplace. The last thing you want is for the owner to find out from someone in the neighborhood about a recent sale, and ask you why *you* didn't tell him first!

All of these steps are key to your having only the kind of listings that give you the opportunity to love your job while helping your sellers through the very emotional experience of trying to sell their home. If done correctly, it will complete your goal of helping to define the seller's behavior and goals.

Be The Captain

Of Your Ship

CHAPTER FOUR

Chapter 4: Be The Captain Of Your Ship

Many times, upon meeting a new client, you want to jump right into the goal of the buyer or seller, i.e. *to buy a home we love* or *to sell the home we own.*

Of course, that's the general goal for buyers and sellers, but if you skip the very important step of asking the right questions, you will be assuming things that may not be true. You may have the common tendency of agents to give a lecture about your town, the home prices, the schools, socioeconomic trends, and many other topics you think they should know about your town, and about you, as their agent. This information will come out as you get to know them better, but first, you must ask the questions about *them* and *their* feelings and opinions.

Newspaper reporters are always taught to ask the 6 most valuable questions: *What?, When?, Where?, Why?, Who?, and How?.* If you want to learn about your buyer clients, you must ask these same questions before rushing out to show a list of homes in a vacuum.

Let's start with the buyer client. Before jumping into your car and meandering through town, it's wise to ask *why* they are thinking of moving. Their answer will tell you a motivation level, and how important and pressing this move is to them. This "why" question will probe their emotional needs for this move. I once had a client with whom I had worked for several weeks before she said they were going on vacation and would be back in touch when they returned. Before our showing was over, she made the remark, "It's getting bad now with the kids playing outside, and the other kids are picking on them again". When I called her a few weeks later, she told me that they were buying a house (with another agent, before we had Buyer Brokerage). The agent had called her about a house that I hadn't shown her and she grabbed it. I was shocked because her two main concerns had been a large dining room and a large master bedroom. The house she was buying had *no* dining room and a *tiny* master bedroom!

Had I known that the situation with her sons being bullied was the most important reason for moving out of her condo, I would have shown her everything available that could close soon. I would have shown her that house she was buying, even though it lacked the two things she had said were imperative. The situation with her kids was ten times more important to her at that moment. Perhaps if I had probed deeper, I would have picked up on the urgency of this need and concentrated on *why* she needed to buy.

Sometimes people will answer the "why" question with reasons like "I want a more prestigious neighborhood" or "I need more space" or "I'm tired of living in chaos and noise, and I want some peace and quiet".

This is a good time to ask *where* they are coming from, and *where* they want to go.

Asking this can give you an idea of the kind of home they are living in and asking *why* will give you even more insight about their motivation.

Asking "*what* are you looking for?" will elicit from them specifics like style of homes they like and dislike, and this will simplify the search. If a client says, "I hate split level homes", you can refine your list more easily. They will also reveal what towns they want to look at, what recreational needs they have, and transportation preferences ("I don't want a long drive to town" or "I want to be able to walk to the train" or "I want to be within 10 minutes of the highway".) Spiritual needs can be determined with gentle questions about what type (if any) religious institutions they want to be near. Sometimes, they will even give clues as to the type of street or neighborhood they are seeking ("I like my privacy and don't want to see neighbors" or "I want my kids to go out and play and walk to their friends' houses").

Now that you know the answers to *what* they are looking for, it's time to get more specific and drill down farther on the other parts of this puzzle.

Find out *who* will be living in the home. Letting them describe their family to you will give you insight as to what they want for this family. Allowing them to expand on this topic will give you better direction in your search to accommodate their needs and wants. For instance, if you discover that they have parents or in-laws who visit frequently from out-of-town, you will want to be sure that there is a place for them to stay on a visit. The client will let you know how important that is to them, or they may say, "My parents always prefer to stay at a nearby hotel." You might find out that one child in the family is a serious musician or dancer and needs a space in the home to practice without being disturbed. The more you let the clients talk, and not try to give them the intensive "orientation tour", the better you will be able to eliminate inappropriate homes for them, and the faster you will find the perfect home for them.

When they want (or need) to move should be taken very seriously. If they say, "I'm in no hurry" it should guide you in the amount of effort you want to put into this work, and you should take your cues from them. When their needs become more pressing, you'll know. They will set the speed with which this search will proceed (or not!) A caution here: Many people are just curious about seeing homes, and they really don't have any pressing reason to buy a home. You can use this question about "when" to help you decide how much time and energy you want to put into this assignment.

One last question to ask is "*How* are they planning to do this move?" Do they have enough money on hand for a down payment? Do they already have a contract on their own home? Would they consider an interim rental if they close on their own home before being able to close on a new home? This is the time to refer them to a professional mortgage person who can help them through this "how" of the transaction. You also need to know these answers before spinning your wheels on clients who have great motivation, share their needs with you, seem to know exactly the kind of home they like, but don't have the financial footing to do this at all. A conversation with the mortgage professional should answer that issue with lightning speed. Then it is your duty to inform the client that they will have to look in a different price range or in a nearby town with lower priced real estate.

This mortgage component should ideally be covered before you ever physically take the client out. What point would there be in traversing the town and show-ing great homes, only to find out that these people can't afford these properties? The mortgage profes-sional knows the right questions to ask and the neces-sary documentation to request so that you don't have to deal with this sensitive information.

I learned all of this the hard way, so I'm sharing with you some ways of asking the right questions before you get too far into a process which may end badly. If you perfect the art of ASKING instead of TELLING, you will be doing three things which will help you:

1) You will get to know so much more about your clients' feelings and true motivation

2) You will be able to judge how probable it is that they will be able to find (and pay for!) the home they love

3) Most importantly, it will help you to stay in charge, like a ship's captain, and not be lashed from wave to wave by an impractical or unmotivated or indecisive client.

There Are

Positive Negatives

CHAPTER FIVE

Chapter 5: There Are Positive Negatives

In a previous chapter, I wrote about toxic clients. You now have an understanding of what that toxicity can do to your self- confidence, and how it can render you less effective with your "good" clients. You are probably nodding, but at the same time thinking, "I can't afford to drop a client." I'm answering, "Yes, you *can*, and *you must*."

The first type of client to think about giving up is the aforementioned toxic client.

These clients are not evil people. They are not setting out to destroy you. They just are not open to listening to you, letting you lead them to the "right" home, keeping scheduled showing appointments, and they are arriving late or canceling frequently. Sometimes, they are just rude, challenging you on everything you say, showing their statistics from the internet, and trying to be "in charge" at all times. This client always needs to be right, and never misses an opportunity to impress you with his knowledge of the real estate market. Every time you prepare a list of homes to show, he will try to see how much you know and whether it says the same thing in an article he just read in a book, magazine, or on a website chart.

Many times, these clients are just not motivated about buying right now. They are in "discovery" mode and, of course, you want to educate them about the market trends and show them some inventory. Others may just be indecisive people in everything they do, not just house hunting. The question for you to ask yourself is, "How long do I want to continue to just ride around showing exteriors and interiors of homes and neighborhoods without seeing any sign that they are getting closer to the house they say they are searching for?" That's always up to you. Remember: *you get to choose whom to work with*, and *you* get to say, "I've had enough; this isn't going anywhere and it's not working!"

Another type client you might consider giving up is the type that refuses to take advice from you. Even though you have experience and skill in negotiating and pricing, this client will not take direction or coaching. I had a client many years ago who was in the multi-million dollar range. I had taken them out for many months, usually on short notice, many times, and they bid on many homes, always 25-30% off the asking price, and never increasing their bids. They kept meeting me at homes, refusing to travel in my car, and not allowing me to travel in their car either. Finally, they found a home they loved, became really excited about it, and made me come into their car for the first time to discuss strategy for an opening bid. This house was very well priced and I counseled them to bid not less than 10% off the price of the home.

They followed my direction, made the bid, and I presented it. The listing agent came back with a counter offer of midway between their bid and the asking price of the home, and also shared that there was another interested buyer.

My client said, "We're off to Montreal for the weekend, and we'll call when we get back." I tried to explain that there was other interest, but he wouldn't continue negotiating. Over the weekend, the owners accepted the other party's offer. When my client got back and called me, I told him that the house had an accepted offer. I also told him that there was nothing more I could do for them in this town, and would rather not work with them anymore. When he asked why,

I recited the list of all of the homes he had seen and had bid low on without raising his bids. I actually felt good about this; I had made my choice and no longer had to feel ineffectual. Two years later they called me again and said that they were really serious now, and asked if I would work with them again. I said yes, and we did reconnect.

In today's digitally intensive market, we have some very savvy people coming to us. These people are used to doing things in a mode that may be alien to some agents, especially those who have been in the business for a long time. In "olden times", the agent controlled all the information, called clients on the phone, and discussed needs, wants, timetables for buying or selling, price ranges, and all other concerns.

Today, our clients come into the office armed with graphs, statistics, examples, photos, and a myriad of other data, which they want you to reply to on the spot!

Here is where you have to quietly sit down with the client and go over the method you will use to help them find the perfect home, and that method must be *your* method.

A number of years ago, I had a young couple walk into the office who "blew into town" without any plans or notice, and wanted me to put together things to show them in about 15 minutes while they went next door to have some coffee and a bite to eat. I was frantic. How could I do this? I would have to research the listings in their range, call the listing agents, make a showing schedule, print out the listings, and orient the clients to our town while driving them around in my car. I'm getting exhausted now, just thinking about that day which was many years ago.

Today, that would never happen to me. Today I would refuse to act like a performing seal. I have expertise, and I need to find out a great deal more about my clients before I take them out and fly around indiscriminately letting them into a list of homes. I would need to ask them all of the questions which I wrote about in the last chapter – "*who, what, where, why, when, and how*" before I would ever take anyone out to see homes. What would be accomplished by running out on a moment's notice?

At any rate, these were clients that that I decided not to work with that day. They were the type of people (under 30 years old, very statistically oriented, and very impatient) with whom I could not establish rapport. I politely told them that, if they could sit down for a while and let me find out some more about them, I would be able to work with them. They didn't have the time or the inclination for that. We parted amicably, and I felt relieved at not having to jump at every new command. I had made the choice to forego this client, and I felt good about it. *Could* you or *would* you do the same? Generational gaps are often the reason that some agents and clients don't "mesh". It's no shame to realize that not every client-agent relationship is a match made in heaven. The point here is, again, you *can* control your client base, and you will *not* capture every prospective client!

A reason that you may lose an existing client and suffer some self doubts is when the client's relative or good friend enters the real estate business. It has happened to me a few times, has happened to many of my colleagues, and it will happen to *you* at least once in your career, if it hasn't happened already. Being able to understand and accept this is key. Many new people enter the business every day, and your former client may feel obligated to this new agent, and drop you.

Maybe his employer's wife just got her license, and he feels pressure from his boss to "give her a chance", and he does. Part amicably, ready for the next opportunity.

You can't capture every listing either. This is an area about which I can speak from experience. In most cases, a potential seller asks you in for a listing presentation. You go to the home, find it cluttered, messy, and really unattractive. You give some advice (diplomatically, of course!), and the seller refuses to listen. They won't consider hiring an organizer and/or a stager. Do you really *want* this listing, or will you decide this is one you will choose not to pursue? Another seller resists your recommendation for a listing price, and demands that the house be listed at *his* price.

This has happened to me several times over the course of my long career in this business. One home that I could not capture as a listing was later listed with another agent at an inflated price, which was much higher than my suggested price. These people were friends of mine, and I had just negotiated a sale for them on a new house that they were buying. Their own home, which they listed with another agent for much too high a price, eventually sold two years later, for much less than the price I had established. Would *you* have flattered them and taken the listing and plodded through two years of stress, or would you have said, as *I* did to myself, "Thank heaven I didn't have to deal with this situation for two years!" (P.S. they are still my friends!)

Another client who was still living in a home I had sold them about 20 years before, listed with another agent who gave them a higher price (or agreed to the price that the seller wanted to ask). They never did sell their home, even though it stayed on the market for about eighteen months. They took it off the market and are still living in it.

If you already have a listing, and the seller keeps making demands on you, is this a situation you want to stay in? Sometimes they demand newspaper ads every week, they severely restrict showing hours, and create impractical showing conditions. This may become very trying and frustrating for you. Have you ever "fired" a client? How bad would things have to become before you would consider doing that?

Another situation that may stop your client's buying process is that he or she loses his employment. They might be ready to sign a contract and then find out they have no job. One of my clients had this very thing happen to him. Luckily, he had a mortgage contingency in the contract, and he was able to get his deposit back. I accepted that this was nobody's fault, and was glad for them that they hadn't signed a non-contingent contract. Similarly, a buyer client thinks his own home will sell, and it doesn't. He then cannot follow through. Also, a client may be coming to your town on a job transfer, but the job transfer gets canceled. These things happen, and you must be prepared to lose some transactions.

One agent just revealed a sad story about how she had worked for many months with a couple looking for a home. These were people whom she had placed in a rental a year before. During that year, she introduced them to others at little coffee meetings at her home, showed them around and took them to many events in the town, and even had her daughter baby sit for their children – in short, she really became their good friend as well as their real estate agent.

When the rental year was coming to an end, they started looking for a home to buy. After many times out looking, they settled on a home, made an offer, haggled for many days through many lowered counter offers from the seller, and finally settled on a price. They scheduled a building inspection, and when the results came in, they haggled some more, wanting a credit for many of the systems and appliances in the house that were still functioning, but would eventually have to be replaced. In our area, that kind of situation usually does not warrant a lowering of an agreed upon price for the home, unless it is a safety issue. They, however, did wear the owner down, and a credit was agreed upon.

When they were to have signed the contract, they backed out of the transaction! They gave no explanation, except to say that they didn't feel enough was done to make the deal worthwhile for them. The agent decided not to work with them anymore. She felt good doing this, as she believed they were not acting in good faith. When she saw them at an event many months later, they sheepishly admitted that they had bought another home (at about *half the price* of the one she was trying to sell them!) The agent now assumes that they could not really afford the first home, perhaps due to a job change or other adverse financial conditions, and were too embarrassed to tell her that. So, you can see that sometimes it is better to walk away, move on, and not continue to be frustrated with clients who do not tell you the truth, for whatever reason.

What type of agent do you want to be? One who hangs in, no matter what or how long?

The main theme of this chapter is to know when to quit. When to say "uncle", and move on to the clients who are more motivated, qualified, realistic in their goals, and in sync with your style of doing business. I repeat: it is always your choice to end anyone's ability to make you feel as though you are not good at what you do.

This business is not a prison; you have great freedom, and sometimes saying "no" will give you that freedom you deserve.

Make It...

The Time Of Your Life

CHAPTER SIX

Chapter 6: Make It The Time Of Your Life

Have you ever thought that a calendar and a clock could actually liberate you? Most of us feel as though we are slaves to calendars and clocks, and could never envision them as instruments to make our lives easier. I actually love dates and time schedules. Instead of them being limiting factors in my life, they are allies. I use them to make some sense of the hectic life of a Realtor, and I can share some of my secrets with you.

Of course, I plan all of my client showings, public open houses for my listings, office meetings, and broker open houses. How could I do my work without it? Everyone realizes the importance of making this a priority, or else how would we function in a business world?

But even the "chores" that come with being a Realtor and are not usually scheduled can be made easier and less stressful with a little planning. Do you have an actual time of day or evening that you block out to do recurring business tasks? Do you know what they are? Are they a regular part of every day? Let's review some of them:

Firstly, do you look at your MLS hot sheet at the same time(s) every day? Is it part of your routine, or do you just "get to it" when you have some free time? Have you actually assigned a specific hour of the day to do this during the workweek? Of course, the hot sheet is not always complete until mid-morning, and then it is updated sometime in the afternoon, after new information is submitted by the agents. Do you make that activity a slot on your daily calendar and review the hot sheet on your computer, tablet or smart phone?

Your own listings must be periodically updated to keep them fresh. Do you do this as a regular practice, or do you just amble through the days and weeks without refreshing the comments on the listings? Do you make it a regularly scheduled routine to investigate the online sites like Zillow, Realtor.com, and Trulia to see what type and volume of activity there is on your listings? Without scheduling a set time to do this, you may get caught short by your client who has made a habit of checking all the sites to see how his house is being advertised. You can be sure the clients make it a regular part of *their* day!

Speaking of clients, when do you call or write to them? Most people would say, "When I have something to tell them." Many of the people who "lose" their existing listings to another agent when the expiration date arrives do so because the seller feels neglected. If you had it on your calendar as a scheduled call or note, your client would feel cared for. Without a written schedule, you probably won't follow through on this. If you choose an hour every day for your "client catch-ups", you won't be at risk of forgetting to contact your clients. If you regularly work out, you don't "forget" to do it. It is penciled into a time slot every day on your calendar, right? You know it's important to you, so you always keep the appointment with yourself to work out, don't you?

I belong to a business network group that meets every week at an early morning hour, and attendance is man-datory. I have that scheduled into my weekly calendar all year long, and it helps me to have that scheduled time to network, and not depend on chance meetings at the supermarket or at school pick-ups. Scheduling actually frees you of the responsibility of finding time in your busy day to do this necessary but elusive task. By writing it into your calendar, you are helping yourself to stay on track with every client. If you choose to email them, make it at a set time every day. If it's early morning or late at night, it won't matter; the clients will read it when they check their messages at a time of their choosing.

Okay, enough of the work time schedule! I think you get the idea, and you may already be doing these things because you learned a long time ago how helpful it is to maintain regular client contact. One of the things I do is to send a very upscale magazine designed for Realtors to send to their clients. It features my photo on the front cover, a short letter by me on the inside front cover, and many interesting articles about American life. This arrives every two months at my clients' homes. It has great shelf life, and I don't have to remember to send something to all of these people because it is scheduled and mailed by the publisher. You may be thinking, "Oh, but it's probably very expensive." Actually, in the scheme of things, it's not prohibitively costly, and one real estate listing or sale would pay for about ten years of this magazine!!!!

What about your *other life* (if you have one!) aside from real estate? If you are in charge of the maintenance of your home because your spouse works farther from home than you do and keeps longer hours, you will probably feel "pinned down" by these responsibilities. If you have the funds to hire people to do this work for you, this would definitely free you up to spend more hours doing your real estate work. If you are not a gardener, and pulling weeds causes you stress and physical pain, hire someone (even a neighborhood teenager) to do this time-consuming chore.

When will you find the time to cook or to shop? This is also where a schedule will help you to manage your home. If you carve out a specific time for these tasks, you can still see clients at any of the other times. It's when you run from errand to errand without a schedule that you become frazzled. Think how much easier it would be to work your clients into your schedule, working around those few hours you have carved out for your own activities! Usually, in this profession, we have to allow more client time on weekends, so why not try to allocate parts of the weekdays for your *other life* schedule?

If you are the designated shopper in your household, it would simplify things if, let's say, every Monday at 12 noon you plan to do your supermarket shopping. When a client wants to see you, you could suggest 10 AM, or 2 PM, or even 4 PM. Have you ever tried that? Do you realize that *you* can be in on the client scheduling, and can offer them several times that *you* are free? The order in your life (and the sense that *you* are also important!) can come from a simple thing like making appointments around your *other life's* scheduled events.

You need to *look* your best and *feel* your best in order to *do* your best job for your deserving clients. That may entail grooming appointments for your hair and nails, and workout sessions or classes that you enjoy. If you schedule them at a regular time each week or each day, you will still have all the other hours in the week to do your professional work – and you will look and feel good doing it! I have always had an appointment for my nails every two weeks at a salon and every month at the hairdresser's for my haircuts. When I need to schedule a client, since those grooming times are already blocked out, I find one of the many unscheduled times to work with the client.

As part of your *other life*, your children will have you running in many directions if you don't make schedules and plans. One of the things that can help is a car pool with nearby parents so that you will be driving only certain days of the week or the month. In our town, many of the children have all sorts of lessons and activities after school, and you could be flying around wildly if you haven't arranged a schedule in advance. With these activities for the kids, you can find many opportunities as well. I met many of the other parents at sports or music events where my girls participated. Yes, it took me away from my desk, but it also allowed me to get to know the other parents and share with them when they asked questions about real estate (as everyone seems to do!) You have regular mealtimes, hopefully, which most people (including clients) have, so you don't usually have to run around showing homes at dinnertime.

Lastly, but just as important, is the appointment you should be scheduling with your spouse or significant other. "What???? Shouldn't that be spontaneous?? How will I fit that into my crammed workweek? If I am working so hard, how can I plan to have fun if I am too tired?" I believe you cannot forget about this most important part of your *other life*. This is the person who will buoy you up with his or her love and attention. This is the well you will drink from to rejuvenate your weary soul. Work is not mainly what your life is about, is it? My husband and I had "date nights" before that term was even invented. We scheduled a baby sitter every week, and went out together to be away from the everyday life (children and work). It was truly one of the best things for our relationship, and helped us to give each other strength and peace. Just one night away from work, chores, and children kept up our enthusiasm for life and nourished our love for each other.

There is one other area that I'd like to mention in this "time of your life" segment, and that is "time off". Have you scheduled any time off lately? By that I mean a bit of time every day, even if it's only a half-hour, where you turn off your computer, cell phone, tablet, and TV. Can you do that? Can you just "chill" totally at a set time every day? Can you just read or listen to instrumental music, or take a long luxurious bath or sit in the sauna? The result of this will be more balance and strength to do better business, and to be healthier and happier. Everyone needs some "down time" every day, and I'm giving you permission to take it. I do this regularly, and people have always remarked about how cheerful and happy I seem to be. I am also generous and, because of that, I am sharing these suggestions with you, my reader.

Try it….you'll like it…I promise!

The Family Is All In

CHAPTER SEVEN

Chapter 7: The Family Is All In

If you are like most real estate agents, you are riddled with guilt about spending weekend time or even meal-time with your clients instead of your family. This, unfortunately, is a by-product of this business, as most clients are more available on weekends than during the week, when they are usually busy with their own children's activities, or else they are at work.

I mentioned in the last chapter that making schedules is key, and how you should try to do some things for yourself and your family. You could try to work around your family commitments but, if that doesn't work, what are you to do? I still remember an incident many years ago when my husband and I were getting ready to go bike riding with our 2 daughters. We were on our driveway, with helmets on and bicycles ready, and then I realized I had forgotten something (I've now forgotten what the forgotten thing was!), and I ran back into the house to get it. Suddenly the phone rang (no cell phones in those years!) and it was a client couple from a nearby state whom I had worked with before. They said they were in town and had clipped out some ads from the New York Times (no internet either in those days!) and wanted me to show them the houses advertised. They said they were already in town and could meet me in about 20 minutes.

I reluctantly agreed and then went back out to the driveway, where my family was waiting. I had to tell them that Mommy just got a client call and could not go cycling with them. I said, "Daddy will take you; I'm sorry." To this day, I can still remember the looks on their faces (all three of them, including my husband!). How disappointed they looked! Needless to say, that couple did not buy any house *that* day, or *any* day, and I could never recapture that opportunity to spend that quality time with my family. I had scheduled this date because we all deserved it and wanted it, and I reneged. I made a vow that day that I would never leave a scheduled family event to respond like Pavlov's dog to a sudden request from a client. I have not broken that promise, and I feel really good about that.

That was an easy decision to make, especially in view of the advice I have given in the chapters *The Time of Your Life* and *Positive Negatives*. Sometimes, however, we do have to schedule clients at times when our families would rather have us with them than out working. How could you ever make this a positive for your children? How do you involve them in your success? What about your spouse's possible resentment of your work during "normal family time", i.e. weekends and holidays?

One method that I used was to reward my children with a gift or special event if they found a new client for me. If they heard one of their friends talking about how their parents are thinking of looking for a new house or saying things about maybe selling their house and moving to another, my daughters would let them know that their mother was a Realtor and could help them. I actually did get a few clients that way, and it resulted in a nice reward for my child. In this way, your child can be a part of your profession, like a referral agent, and will not always resent the time spent away from them.

Another way that your family can help to contribute to your success without feeling resentment is for them to do some work for you. With the advent of the computers, and the children's ease with its many functions, they can usually surpass your capabilities. They can assist with charts, graphs, creating flyers, and so many things that come so easily for them, but which are sometimes daunting to us. Again, there was no internet for the first 25 years that I was in this business, but my girls were still engaged in helping me by addressing, sealing, and stamping envelopes. This helped me, but, more importantly, it involved them in an activity that they would otherwise resent for taking their mother's time from them. The could actually learn what sometimes keeps me from spending more time with them, and see this process close up, and give it a name. Instead of this being an unknown threat, they could see some of my work duties and be proud that they were helping me.

Rewarding them monetarily does two things for them: (1) it shows them that they can earn some money for making your life easier and (2) it can motivate them to listen for clues from their friends' parents who may need your help in a real estate situation. If and when you do sign up the listing contact, a financial reward can go a long way in teaching your child that being your "referral agent" or your tech "guru" is appreciated. When my daughter was instrumental in my getting the listing of her friend's home, and the home sold, she got a part of that commission as a gift. There's nothing like a concrete reward to help children embrace being part of your work life!

Now, for the spouses: I was so fortunate with my husband's attitude toward my profession. He was my biggest fan, and truly "the wind beneath my wings", as Bette Midler so perfectly described in her hit song of the same name. In fact, I was so moved by those words, that I once gave him the CD as a Valentine's Day gift! He was always my proudest cheerleader, and really applauded every success that I had through the many years in this business. He bought me flowers every time I had a closing! This kind of support is invaluable in a Realtor's life.

Unfortunately, for some agents, they will experience great resentment from a spouse who dislikes the hours spent away from him or her. In some cases they can even be jealous if you become so successful that your earnings are higher than theirs. In the worst cases, a spouse can become so upset with your work that he or she will find ways to sabotage it. In an ideal relationship, your spouse will become your greatest support system and do things to make you even more successful.

Having dealt with the spouses of my agents when I owned my real estate company, I have seen all manner of resentment and downright sabotage. This certainly did not aid the agents in their careers. Just having the peace of mind knowing that your spouse or significant other is in your corner and serves as your best cheerleader can do wonders for an agent.

One of the things which is so simple for him or her to do is to always carry a few of your business cards. One never knows when he will meet someone who is looking to buy or sell a home. If he truly cares about aiding you in your business, he will offer the person your card if they mention their quest for a new home or their unhappiness in their in their present home. This supportive spouse will not keep your profession a secret from his co-workers. On the contrary, he or she will find a way for the person to know that they can count on you to work for them or to refer them to an agent in the town they are moving from or the town in which they wish to find a home.

Your spouse can help you in many social ways as well. You may want to show gratitude to a client who has closed a deal with you. If your husband or wife will join you in taking them out to dinner, it will be a much warmer occasion than if you had to do it alone. My husband did this for me with many of my client appreciation dinners. If I had them to my home for dinner or to a party for a group of clients, he was always a willing participant, joining in the conversations and helping with the bar. Unfortunately, my husband passed away a few years ago, so I have to do these dinners or parties by myself, and they are not nearly as much fun. In fact, now dinners out can be awkward, as the client couple is sometimes embarrassed to let a single woman pay!

Another great favor your spouse can do for you is to be a sounding board for your upcoming listing presentations. By letting you "rehearse" and giving you a critique, he is helping you to have your actual presentation polished. Also, he or she can review flyers, letters, and any other written materials you plan to distribute. Just another pair of eyes can make a fairly good product into an excellent one. Doing this together can also allow him or her (just as it did with the children) to see what you are working on which might be taking time away from him or her. By being a part of your work, he or she is becoming an even more important ally. When you do get the client, your spouse will feel invested in this and *your* success will also be *their* success.

With your having to work many weekends, the spousal cooperation in the children's activities is such a necessary component and it is critical that you know you can rely on this. Let's say you have to meet a client at 2 PM on a Sunday, and your husband usually likes to watch football on TV at that time. His cooperation is key to your children having a fun time and not blaming you for a boring day. Your spouse should, ideally, take up the slack and play a game with them or take them out to the park or a movie, or, at the very least, invite the children to watch the game with him. With older children who don't drive yet, your spouse should be available, willing, and even happy to take them out to an activity in which they want to participate.

The conversation about these weekend conflicts is ideally one which you should have *before* you decide to enter the business. My team leader mentioned to me that when someone wanted to join his previous firm, the owner of the firm required the spouse to come in for an interview with the prospective agent. This was done to prepare the spouse for what was ahead, and to see if he or she was on board with it. It's too late and will cause a lot of unnecessary stress for you, the children, and the spouse if it is just sprung on him or her when the occasion arises. This is very much a predictable situation, and it should be discussed thoroughly when you sit down with your spouse and children at the beginning of your real estate career. If your spouse plans something special for the times you will be with clients, the kids will hardly notice that you're not there, and you'll be able to give your full attention to the clients you are working with at that time.

I think you can see why this chapter was given the name "The Family is All In". In this case, it may not take a village, but it surely does take a family!

Forget Me Not

CHAPTER EIGHT

Chapter 8: Forget Me Not

In the course of over 30 years that I have been in this profession, I may have lost a client or two, but it was *never* because they *forgot* me! Perhaps someone close to them just joined the field, and they felt they had to give this person a chance. Perhaps they became a Realtor themselves (it does happen, more often than you think!) Perhaps they belong to a club or book group or other networking groups and they have met an agent there and see him weekly or monthly. All of these reasons, though not particularly uplifting, are tolerable and understandable. The reason I never want to hear is *I forgot you were in the business* or *it's been so long that I wasn't sure you were still active in real estate* or, worse than that, *I couldn't find your card, and I forgot your name*. I did not make these things up; I have witnessed so many agents losing clients for the simple reason that the clients did not remember them or were unsure if the agent was still around.

Of course, you can mitigate this problem greatly by being sure to follow up after a closing on a regular basis or by being sure to "check in" with a semi-active buyer client frequently. How could they forget you if you do this routinely?

One of the things I invest in is the bi-monthly magazine I mentioned in an earlier chapter. The publisher has a filtering system that ensures that no other Realtor can send the publication to any registered client of mine. This avoids confusing duplicates a client might receive, and keeps this list as your own protected client mailing. I choose about 50 past, present, or prospective clients who I think would enjoy it. It is personalized with their name in the inside cover letter, and my name is prominently displayed in several places in the magazine as well as on the cover. I regularly edit the list of recipients as they "defect", move out of the country, or become "non-starters" after a significant time period. This is my way of being sure that the people in my *sphere of influence* do not forget me, and I don't have to worry about my forgetting to send something every couple of months. The great part about this is that it has "shelf life" (pardon the pun, but the recipients do save these magazines I send, and they even tell me that they do!)

For those clients who are young and primarily reading online, you may want to find a suitable e-magazine to send out every few months. It won't have the staying power that a hard copy magazine has, but it can be better than nothing for the clients who avoid printed periodicals.

In addition to this regularly scheduled periodical, I am always on the lookout for timely articles in newspapers and magazines that would benefit my contacts. This is usually done by email as an attachment when I see something pertinent to certain clients in my list. (This list is very specific to each possible article, usually not "one size fits all"). Many times I get wonderful responses to these helpful articles or charts or whatever I decide to send. Another way that I stay in touch with my clients and former clients is to send them any news of new listings or sales on the street or in the neighborhood where they live. They see that I remember them, and that I am aware of what's going on in their area. When was the last time you sent out an interesting piece of mail to some of the people on your client list?

Another forget-me-not tool is to be sure to call on the phone occasionally. I know this is becoming harder to do in this age of smart phones and other electronic communication devices, but it is still worth the time and effort to connect this way, particularly because it is so rare. When they hear your voice, it gently reminds them that you're still thinking of them, and they can react to your cheerful (hopefully!) voice and message to them. Sometimes, they actually answer the cell call!! This becomes truly a unique experience, since so few agents bother to do it anymore. You will stand out amid a deluge of written text messages and emails that they receive from everyone else in their life.

If you want to make a really standout communication, try sending them a "snail mail" card or letter (not a mass produced one done by a printer! They sometimes get one or two of these from others once in a while). What I am suggesting is a note in *your handwriting* (you do still know how to write with a pen, right?) that is directed to them only. Say something personal; mention something about one of their kids.

You know what to do. You used to do these things, but you gave up on this way of connecting a while ago.

When I see anything (photo or name mentioned) about them or their children, I clip it from the place where I found it, and send it with a note marking the importance of this event. I have actually gotten listings by doing this, as the client was so flattered that I remembered their child and recognized his accomplishments in a written letter with the article or photo enclosed. Sometimes you will see an article about their neighborhood or one about a club or group that you know they belong to – do you send a copy to them, or do you just skip over it?

This is a very easy thing to do, and it will separate you from the herd, and help your clients to feel really good about you.

As a way of not letting your special clients forget you, it is a very lovely gesture to make a party at your home and invite past clients, present clients, and, if applicable, the people who referred them to you. Speaking of that last group, do you remember to acknowledge each referring person with a token of your appreciation? If there is someone who thought enough of you to send you a friend, colleague, or relative, don't you want him to do it again? One way I have done this is to have a New Year's Day open house or a January Sunday Brunch for all of my clients from that past year. An invitation to my home is a very personal, friendly way of showing them that they are important to me. Perhaps you belong to a country club and would rather do this party or dinner there. That's great if you can afford it, but, if you are on a budget, a home party can be done on a smaller scale and is just as meaningful.

After a client closes on a home, do you consider your job done, or do you continue to be their agent by giving them a long- lasting gift that will remind them of you whenever they look at it? This is also true for the seller of a home who is your client. I have given fireplace equipment, gift certificates for mailboxes, and paintings of their house done on canvas or on serving platters. Every time they look at or use the item, they will remember you fondly. They may even have guests who admire the item and ask where they got it. The answer will be "my real estate agent gave it to me."

Doesn't that sound like a good idea? Theater tickets, gift certificates, and flowers are lovely, but will they be a lasting and meaningful reminder of you and your service to them every time they use it? One gift, which

I have been giving to all of my clients who close on a house with me, is a beautiful four-color woven afghan with scenes of our town all over it. Buyers love it for showing them many of the landmarks in town, and sellers love it as a reminder of their time in our town. They take this afghan to their new home and nostalgically think of their former town. The added feature in this particular gift is that it was created by a local service group, and buying the afghan is a way of making a donation to a worthwhile cause. If your town doesn't have such an item, you might want to inquire about how to get one crafted by a local artist for a local charity to sell. I have come into the new homes of my past clients, and the afghan is still being used and proudly displayed for all of their visitors to see.

Having your new clients to your home for dinner may seem like a labor-intensive chore, but it is so special because, like the hand-written note, it is rarely done. The food does not have to be gourmet caliber, and your home doesn't have to be a palace; it's just that you are sharing some*thing* you care about with some*one* you care about. When was the last time *you* did this? The best part about this gesture is that you will enjoy it as much, if not more, than your invited clients. The ideal small group to invite would be one couple that already bought with you and one who is working with you now or just bought a home. Your past client will do the praising of you, and you come out looking like a winner. They will also be able to name lots of interesting places and events that they enjoy in town and, coming from someone other than the agent, it will be appreciated by the new client.

When the closing is long past, even years ago, it's so nice to schedule periodic visits to the home they bought. Regular visits are reminders that you care about them and their family, and it helps to keep you in the forefront of their mind so that the next time they are asked whom they used as a Realtor by a prospective buyer or seller, there will be no hesitation in recalling your name and how much they like you.

All of these memory-joggers do work. As I said in the first sentence of this chapter, they may not always use you as their agent the next time, but it will never be because they forgot who you are! You can keep yourself clearly in their minds and heart, and have a head start toward repeat business.

Avoid The
April Showers

CHAPTER NINE

Chapter 9: Avoid The April Showers

It never ceases to amaze me that many people who are real estate agents have still not learned that they are spending what is not legally theirs. These same people would not go into someone's home and steal something because they like it. They would not go to a store and pocket something that doesn't belong to them just because, for a moment, they could handle it and pretend it was theirs to enjoy. It seems pretty basic that upstanding people do not steal what isn't theirs. They save for the things they want, and they buy those things when they can afford to.

Yet, this lesson is so lost on many independent contractors (not just real estate agents). Independent contractors get paid directly, not from company funds. They get a check (or bank deposit) for 100% of what they earned. It's quite a giddy feeling to be handed a sum of $25,000 at one time or have it electronically deposited into your bank account. This is especially true if it has been a long time since you last had a closing, and that $25,000 is such a welcome treat! Have you set up a special savings account for the part of that money that isn't yours? You do realize that every commission you earn must be shared with an entity that you'd rather not think about, right?

Depending on your income bracket, 28%, 33%, etc. of that money belongs to the U.S. government, in the form of taxes. If this concept stings, and you don't like to be reminded of it every time you earn a commission, you will be crying every April when you have to find that money that you should have been saving and have already spent elsewhere. The concept is so simple, yet I see so many agents in a frantic state every April when the final tax payment is due, and they are looking for ways to find the money to pay it.

Managing our finances is nothing new for many of us, but, somehow, when we came from other professions which were salaried and our companies or schools or government agencies deducted taxes from the paychecks we received, it was something we may have grumbled about, but at least we didn't have to remember to do it ourselves.

I have found that a separate "tax" account in a savings plan is the best way to be prepared to pay your expected share to the government. If your check is $25,000, at least $7500 should immediately be put away and not touched. Not touched??? "But I earned it!!!" "I need it now, for a vacation I scheduled for next month." "My son's college tuition is due in a week, and I don't know when my next commission is coming!" "I had an unexpected large medical bill this past month, and now I have $25,000 at my disposal and I can pay it."

WRONG!! That money is not all yours! We do not live tax-free in this country, and, sooner or later, you will be billed for the amount you owe.

I know this sounds simplistic and, for many, it may be an unnecessary topic to be discussing now. However, you'd be surprised at the stress level that this money management (or lack thereof) causes many independent contractors, but, especially for this book, I am primarily talking about Realtors. How does one balance the necessity of dressing well and looking successful to one's clients and the general public with not overspending and using money that we temporarily "steal" from a fund that we should be adding to on a regular basis? This is an ongoing dilemma, as a salesperson has to be able to market himself or herself, look successful, drive a nice car, spend on personal grooming and all the other things to give the public the impression that he or she is doing well in the business.

Therein lies the dilemma; you need the money now for things to keep up a lifestyle, but you'll have to "pay the piper" later, especially in April for the final tax installment. If you don't want to be in tears and, worse, have to take out a loan to pay your taxes, I suggest opening this "hands off" account and deducting 30% from every commission all year long to deposit there. The kind of anxiety caused by not doing this very basic step will manifest itself to your clients very easily, and show up in your demeanor and, perhaps, start to make them doubt you.

The first step in this procedure is to actually make a written budget. Do you know, without looking at your bank accounts and credit card statements, what you actually spend every year? I have done this and was so surprised to see the things I spend money on. Until you really devote some time and energy to this project, you won't understand where "your" money (including the part you should be saving for taxes) is going.

Realtors have to pay quarterly estimated income taxes, predicting what you expect to earn in the next 3 months. Of course, a good CPA will do this with you (for a fee) and set you up on a course to be compliant with the law. If you are diligent about keeping that separate tax account, and you take off 30% of each commission to deposit there, when tax time comes around, there will be no tears, no nail biting, no upset stomachs. If you can whisper to yourself with each commission, "It's not all mine", this needless anxiety will not plague you every 3 months.

A budget can be a real eye-opener if you've never done one before. When I was a salaried teacher, my life was so structured that I knew exactly what I would earn every month, as my deductions were already taken out of my paycheck. I might have overspent here and there, but at least my yearly taxes were accounted for and, some years, I even got a tax refund! Since becoming a Realtor, I have had to be so disciplined at "shaving off" the estimated amount from every earned commission so that I didn't have the April showers of tears. I needed to write this particular chapter in this book because I had, at one point, 20 agents working for me, and I had to listen to many of them crying.

I had to watch them wringing their hands trying to figure out where to get the money to pay the final tax installment in April. We are, as a rule, very creative people in the field of real estate, but sometimes we have to be practical, too. It may not be as much fun to structure a spending budget as it is to prepare a listing presentation or to take beautiful photos of a home you just listed, but it is just as important to your well-being and ultimate happiness. April will come every year, and being ready for it can make the difference between sunshine and showers in your attitude.

Just for fun, try to craft a budget for your own spending patterns. Don't forget clothes, gifts, dining out, entertaining clients, grooming (hair, nail salon) and, of course, your daily lattes. Then get to the "unsexy" stuff like mortgages, rent, groceries, health care, college tuition, home maintenance (gas, oil, electricity, snow removal). I was totally astounded to see on paper the things I spend money on! Luckily, I don't feel comfortable spending on things I don't have money for, but it still was quite a startling exercise to list all of the many items that are in my yearly budget. If you haven't already done this, I advise you to do it very soon. There will be an April this year, and I want you to feel secure and prepared for it. There will be no April showers for your soul if you plan ahead and stick to your plan.

Ready, Set, Goal

CHAPTER TEN

Chapter 10: Ready, Set, Goal

In the last chapter, I talked about saving enough for taxes. In order to have enough income to pay for all the expenses in your newly created budget, you have to set some goals for yearly earnings.

How do we do that? Once you have a budget on paper, line item style, you have a very good idea of what income you will need yearly to be able to meet those expenses. Let's assume that you need $100,000 per year; broken down, that is $8333 per month.

Do you know how you can earn that amount? What can you do to make that goal easier to realize?

You can go back to the closings and rentals that you've done for the past few years. If the average price home you sold was $800,000, the selling or listing portion of that commission (at 5%) was $20,000. This amount, of course, will be shared with your firm at whatever percentage your "split" is. Let's say your split is 55%. That will net you $11,000 gross income before taxes. In order to realize your goal of $100,000 annually, you would have to sell 9 homes of $800,000 per year. Does that sound realistic to you? Have you ever analyzed this before?

If you don't think you can sell 9 homes of $800,000 each, what can you do to reach that $100,000 goal?

There are 2 ways of actualizing this goal. Firstly, you can sell only 4 homes if they are about $1,600,000 each, or you can sell 18 homes at about $400,000 each. Of course, you can't concentrate on only one price range, can you? But you can have a goal for the year, and figure out the best way to arrive at that earning level with an attainable mix of price ranges. If you have never thought about this before, you may be one of those agents who are desperate, unhappy, stressed and clueless as to making a plan to be financially secure by itemizing goals and creating ways to reach them.

Of course, if you can manage your lifestyle on $50,000 a year in earnings, you have an easier target. That's only $4166 per month (before taxes) and can be achieved by selling only 4 homes of $800,000, or 8 homes of $400,000, or even 2 homes of $1,600,000, or any combination which will yield $4166 a month.

It's not that exciting for us to sit and do these kinds of exercises, is it? We like the flair of seeing lovely homes and furnishings, meeting interesting people, getting to know clients, possibly writing ads or taking photos, and all the other "fun" activities that made us want to go into this business in the first place. Working with figures and pre-planning our earnings is somewhat alien to us. We'd rather "wing it" and enjoy the ride. That works only if you have no budgetary concerns and can do this job no matter what you earn. Most of us are not in that enviable position, so we have to learn methods for financial goal setting.

How will we get those 8 or 4 or even 2 sales per year if we don't establish workable steps to get there?

Just as we broke down the income needed per month and year, we can quantify the number of ways we can get a good client base to help us achieve those goals:

How many phone calls per day? How many letters or cards sent each week? How many social events to attend and meet people who might become your clients or who might refer their friends and family members to you? How many posts or blogs will you put on social media sites to establish yourself as an expert in your field?

Yes, these necessary activities can be quantified the same way as you do when you want to set goals for losing weight or gaining more physical strength. You establish how many calories per day you will consume in order to lose 10 pounds. You map out your workout plan with how many minutes on the treadmill or bicycle, how many stretches and sit-ups, how many miles to walk in order to lose those same 10 pounds. Now I am asking you to make a similar "map" of how many homes you need to sell and how many activities you need to do how many times per day and week in order to meet your income goal.

If you don't have a goal, or don't establish the means to reach a goal, you probably won't get there. Just as people "fall off the wagon" in certain self-help programs, you will be floundering around trying to catch your next dollar instead of staying on target with concrete things to do to reach your desired income level.

I told you in the beginning of this book that I see many unhappy people in this profession. Some of them are distressed because they can't seem to make enough money to meet their expenses. They may have success in many of the other areas covered in this book, but the money factor constantly worries them and creates a harried individual. I'd like to see more agents who have a handle on their finances and can be unburdened in this part of their life.

A budget, a goal, and a plan to get there is my answer to this problem. So go to your books and accounts right now and get started on this project…you should see results that will please you by the end of the year.

CHAPTER ELEVEN

Chapter 11: Play Nicely

Remember when you were young and you got together with a few other kids, and your parents always gave you the warning to *play nicely* or you'd have to come home and lose the chance to play with others? Sometimes they used that phrase to tell you and your siblings that they expected you to get along with each other and not fight over silly stuff. You may even have heard that warning when you tried to roughhouse with your dog and your parents stepped in to curb your behavior.

It's too bad that as adult Realtors some of us slip into the childlike bullying and tantrums and one-upmanship that were the hallmarks of youth and adolescence. We work in a community of Realtors totaling about 1,000 in our town in the Multiple Listing Service. Many firms have 50-80 agents in their individual offices, and it would be nice to have a respect and cooperation among all of the agents. This would certainly contribute to a happy life as a Realtor. Alas, this is not always the case. Some agents become so enmeshed and focused on selling a home that they forget basic manners in dealing with other people.

Earlier in this book I wrote of some clients who need to feel as though they are completely in charge of the entire real estate transaction. Well, it's sad to say, but a few agents already have the reputation of being "difficult" to deal with. When the agent on the "other side" of the transaction realizes that he or she has to deal with "that one", undoubtedly tension sets in even before any agreement is achieved. If you look around your real estate community, I'll bet that you can name the 10 or 15 agents who "spell trouble". Why is it that, if given the question, "Who in our real estate community is the most difficult to deal with?" the answers on most lists would probably be the same people?

For some of these troublesome people, the way that they manifest their surliness is shouting, sometimes accompanied by hand gestures. Others make threats. Still others pull rank if they are long-term veterans in this business, and they belittle the less experienced agents with whom they deal. When it comes to negotiating with others, they forget childhood warnings to *play nicely*, and they verbally pummel the weaker or less experienced Realtors. That, of course, clouds the happy life of the other agent in her work environment, and perhaps in her overall feelings of self-worth.

Once in my career, I was actually tricked by another agent. I had a listing of a home I had sold to a family about two years earlier. They had decided that the location wasn't suiting them and they wanted to move closer into town. The asked me if they could put their own ad in the New York Times since I had the exclusive right to sell their home. They felt that an ad by an *owner* might get them more inquiries than a *broker* ad. I allowed it, and another agent called them in response to the ad and said that they should put this home on the Multiple Listing Service. They told the agent that it already was on MLS, and she proceeded to coach them in how to cancel the listing with me. They were told by her to plead that they decided the whole selling ordeal was too much for them. They called me and asked for a cancellation letter (the first and only one in my career!), I signed the letter, and a half hour later there was their house as a new listing with one of those bulldozing agents we all know. I was too trusting, and this other agent was not playing nicely. I am happy to report that this incident is the only one in which I personally have experienced unscrupulous behavior from another agent in our town. I guess that's a pretty good record!

Many times, these aggressive agents forget that they are supposed to act as conduits in a sale of a property, and they are not the *principal players*. In their self-centered manner, they bring tension and rancor into the deal. Instead of guiding a buyer and a seller to the "safe waters" of a compromise on price, closing date, terms of a contract, and other elements of a transaction, they argue their client's side and create friction and enmity that has no place in what could and should be an amicable agreement between two parties.

What can you do about this? Well, one of the things that you shouldn't do is to argue back. Instead, I have found it beneficial to ask for all of the concerns to be written out with the understanding that you will present these concerns to your client. When one of these adult bullies tries to intimidate you and show you the "error of your ways", you can lessen the volume and poison of this harangue by simply lowering your own voice to a barely audible level and asking for these concerns to be written and submitted to you to review with your client.

I remember a rather elderly broker whom I met in my town when I first came into the business. I had a negotiation with her and was so surprised by her terse answers. She reminded me of the detective on the old TV series, "Dragnet" who kept saying, "Just the facts, ma'am, just the facts." This real estate doyenne would answer me in monosyllables and yet was getting the job done. We did reach an agreement, although there was not much "chitchat" involved. Though she had seniority in our real estate community, she just got to the facts as simply as she could, reported them to her client, and came back with an unemotional counteroffer. I was slightly cowed by her "all business" manner but, on reflection, I can see that she was just fulfilling her role as a conduit.

Today, in a somewhat tight real estate market, as my office leader often says, "When the pie gets smaller, the table manners get worse." We have just come through a few years of a really difficult climate in the real estate world and witnessed the very poor manners of some of our fellow agents. Perhaps they were desperate to make a sale and all of the pent up frustration of their situation was leveled at the other professionals they dealt with in their transactions.

We can't always change someone else's behavior, but surely it would be helpful to learn how to protect ourselves from overbearing, impolite, and uncaring members of our sales community. In trying to create a happy life in this field, it would be beneficial to all of the well behaved, polite, and caring people who call themselves Realtors if they could hold their heads up high and keep their volume low and ignore those who darken their days. By not shouting back, you will have the bully ranting to himself and eventually ceasing the assault.

Fortunately, most of us do know how to play nicely and, in doing so, we love what we do and we generally like our co-workers very much. "Into every life a little rain must fall", but mostly it's sunny, and we have so many nice people as our colleagues whom we love to be working with. The next time another agent starts to do a bullying act, try saying, "Just the facts, please; just the facts."

Afterword: What's Next?

We do live in interesting times, and we all should rejoice about that. I have tried to illustrate in this book the many ways that we, as real estate professionals and independent contractors, can enhance our lives by doing things to make us happier human beings.

I have learned some of these things over many years and through many experiences, good and not so good. The important thing is that I did learn them, and, I hope, in my own way, I can be of help to my colleagues in this exciting but sometimes frustrating field.

I love what I do, and I do what I love. What could be better? I wish you, dear reader, success in your life, your whole life, not just your business life. I want to see more smiles and more mirth. I have a feeling that if you can use any of the hints found in these pages, you will see those results. Here's to a rich and happy future for all.

Excelsior!

About the Author

Sandi Klein, GRI, ABR, has been a Realtor in Greenwich, Connecticut since 1975. She was an owner of a successful "boutique" real estate firm for 14 years, opting to sell it to a multi-office chain in 1997. She is currently associated with Berkshire Hathaway Home Services of New England. She has written several children's books, and does frequent copy writing of brochures and home advertisements for fellow agents in her company. Sandi has lived in Greenwich for 40 years, and is an active broker who loves the business and, yes, she has a life!

15783753R00078

Made in the USA
Middletown, DE
21 November 2014